Heartsongs

from a cowboy's soul

by Joe Robinsmith

with special guest

Colton Robinsmith

---

joe.robinsmith@live.ca

http://heartsongs6201.blogspot.com

Dedication

This book is dedicated to my daughter Hailey and my son Colton.

You have been an inspiration since the day you were born. You are both so different and yet so much alike. I loved you both long before you were born. Your joys, your struggles, I have shared even though I have not always been able to be at your side.

My love for you will never die. Though others may come and go in our lives, you will always be my first loves.

Foreword

By Joe Robinsmith

I have new friends both on Facebook and on my blog, Since becoming more focused on my writing, friends who are writers and authors are what I have attracted. Dave Ponder, you were right, increasing my writing energy attracted Sonia Roman, Stephen J Earley, Dave Ponder, Amanda Mathews, Rachel Benson and I already knew the talented D.B. Frank.

I was reading a blog the other day about an author and her WiP. I was like what the heck is she talking about? Then it occurred to me, "Work in Progress". She was referring to her manuscript and her internal editor.

This morning it popped into my head: Wait a minute, there is a huge simile there; we are all, every last one of us, Works in Progress! Wow, what a concept. We are all self-editing our personalities, our friends, our jobs, our lives, our children. We keep adjusting, re-working, editing. Therefore, every person is an artist, and the canvas, the manuscript you are working with/on is you. Some of us manage that pretty well. Some of us don't. Some of us need help with it; we turn to friends, co-workers, counselors, drugs and alcohol even. Whatever we use, it can never replace the fact that we can really only edit ourselves. We can ask for others to review what we have done, but in the end, it is up to each and every one of us to self-edit before submitting that final work to His desk for approval.

Will You

Chorus:
Will you be my best friend
Will you be my lover
Will you walk beside me
Forsake me for no other

Wrap your arms around me
Press your lips to mine
Lay beside and hold me
Until the break of dawn

Never felt this feeling
Never so connected
Universe is pulling
Our two hearts together

Chorus:

When I'm down on one knee
Asking you to marry me
I want you to know this truth
It's 'til the end of time

Forever's not just a word
It's the tie between two hearts
Will you spend eternity
Sharing all your love with me.

Chorus repeat:

The Flower in the Man

The stars in the skies above
Glittered like drops falling
From an ice sculpture left out
Too long

The slivered crescent of a moon
Smiled down on the two lovers
Walking hand in hand along
The beach.

As the waves rolled in to shore
That middle aged man looked up
Smiled at God's grace and spoke,
"Thank you."

She turned and took his face
Looking deep into his eyes
She kissed his lips and eyes
Whispered.

"I wouldn't have you any other way
You're both the flower and the man,
What a beautiful combination.
I SEE you."

The tears rolled down his cheeks
His heart it overflowed
For now it was so obvious
He WAS.

Be yourself with open soul
Live in the moment be alive
Let your heart be true to
Heaven's Light.

Blue Fire

Falling into that bright blue sea

Diving forward I gasp out loud

Eyes close involuntarily.

Your lips curl into a smile

My head a-whirl with giddiness

The light sparkles from your blue eyes

Chorus:
Lady fill my soul with fire

Can't see anyone else but you

Fill my soul with your desire

I only want to be with you

Cowboy's lady so very hot

I only want to be with you.

Your hair is dancing red 'n' gold

Fingers sliding through your soft curls

Sunlight flashing makes my heart bold

Running fingertips up your arm

Your skin so silky smooth and soft

Lovin' knowin' I'm safe from harm

Chorus:

Your healing touch my heart's content

I'm safe within your loving arms

Never had love so permanent

I gaze into your deep blue eyes

Falling into that bright blue sea

So hard to believe you're really mine

Chorus:

Heart's desire, yearning fire

Sunlight dancing through golden hair

The Bigger Picture

There is a George Strait song currently playing
On the radio, JRFM 93.7
Every time I hear that song, I think
That's how my life should be.

Life's not the breaths you take
But the moments that take your breath away

I nod, I laugh, I smile and sing along
I look at my son riding in the truck
Thinking how much like me he has become
I wonder how and why time flew by.

It's not the little things we do
But how we do them every day

My little girl stands there calling
Holding out the telephone
Work is calling daddy, they want you
To come in this weekend.

I nod my head and take the phone
I listen then politely I decline
I only see my little ones
Every other weekend, not today sir. No sir.

I can't believe how fast they've grown
How I wish I could turn back time

Life gets more complicated
Every single day.
But it's not how we handle that stress
It's how we love and hug.

It's not the breaths you take
Not the breathing in and out.
It's the bigger picture it's what it's all about.
I love my little ones now become young adults.

I have made some mistakes along the way
I've shed my share of tears
I've broken hearts and shattered dream
Including that one inside of me.

It's held together by the thinnest threads
Connecting other hearts
Just one lets go and then we fall apart
I'd comfort you, wrap my arms about

If I thought that you'd want me to
Because it's not the past we've had
But how we make each day count.
How can I make it up to you dear heart.

It's not the breaths you take
It's the smiles we share and hugs we give
It's the little ones we care about
That wrap out hearts in love.

Fractured

I've been running scared for so long
Head down and trying hard to hide.
Just don't know how long I've been
Running down the road to hell.

Going nowhere fast those days
Seems like my life has got no meaning
How far is it until the end of time
When I can finally stop running.

And then the Light entered my heart
I thought I was born again and whole
Was moving through a different place
Time was speeding up too fast though.

I was spiraling down into the darkness
I felt so lost and alone, my being shot
Whenever we were apart, I lost it
There was so little light and connectedness.

Wanting you to be safe and warm
Not fractured and focused on another
My heart was yearning to have you near
My soul was aching to ease your fear.

How can we both complete the tasks
That the Light has led us here to do
We cannot repeat the same mistake
Ignore the Light at perils fate.

My soul fractures and splits apart
As I have to leave you there behind
Wishing I could whisk you away
To the place that is ours together.

Fractured is how I feel most of the time
When you are there and I am here.
I feel shut out and abandoned
How I wish I could heal my heart alone.

I need you in my life forevermore
Want your head upon my chest
No need to be cold and alone
No longer either of us fractured and apart.

Dreaming of You

The love that surrounds your heart is sent across the night sky
My thoughts of us fill my mind and soul
I wrap my arms around your memory
And hold you close your cheek
Against my own.
Warmth
Love
Feelings that surround me wake me from sleep
I sit up and see you standing there
Beside the bed I feel you
Your voice calls
My heart
Beats
Fast
How can it seem so real, yet talking to you I know
It was just a wish, a dream, hoping you were close
I lay back down and close my eyes
There is no sleep this morns light
My heart rate high
My thoughts wild
Wishing
Dream
Love.

Magic Happens

When I walked in through that door
I felt the magic in the air
Your eyes invited me for more
And how quickly we went there.

To that place where two hearts connect
From talking on the telephone
Holding hands and talking ‘bout next steps
We didn’t want to be alone.

A love story in the making
The recent past is history
Today a gift for taking
To make a future still a mystery.

Your eyes of green sparkle at me
Makes my heart go pitter patter.
When your fingers brushed my knee
Nothing else seemed to matter.

Your lips so soft against my own
Fingers tracing across your cheek
My heart will never be alone.
Magic in the air as we speak.

Simple Man

I have a simple goal in life
To be the best damned dad I can
Raising my son and daughter
To respect the living land

I never understood
All the anger and the shouting
When we say it's over
Time to start looking for an out.

If you find another love
You better make damned sure
That your heart is ready
And the life you'll lead is pure.

Chorus:
'Cause I am a simple man
There's nothing I want more
Than to live this life I have
True to my inner core.

And when she smiles at you
Across a crowded room
You better be prepared
To fly as high as the moon.

Walking on sunshine
Giving life all you can
She gives you wings to fly
Makes you a better man.

I can't understand sometimes
Why life has to be so hard
But I'll accept the curve balls
And make my last stand.

Chorus:

She gives you wings to fly boy
Be prepared to be a better man
A better man.

She gives you wings to fly boy
Be prepared to be a better man
A better man.

From The Ashes (Phoenix Rising)

The phoenix rests up on it's egg
Contemplating life and death
How certain we contemplate
The beginning and the end.

The end is near so it seems
The tendrilled flames do erupt
Wings spread and beak open
The phoenix lifts its' fiery head

The egg itself remains unscathed
The shell of burnished gold
Flames encircle and entice
The phoenix to remain afoot.

Slowly turning, spinning round
The regal bird with raging eyes
Enraptures my heart and soul
Within it's heart and draws me in.

Together we rise from ashes black
Circling round the nested egg
With one last look around
The phoenix doth disappear.

I'm left a-next the nest
With tears streaming down
They wash away the soot
Revealing cracks across the shell

From within the gleaming gold
A small one emerges seeking air
Fiery wings climb out of the egg
And with piercing eye rebirth occurs.

I am that phoenix, that fiery bird
Emerging from within my shell
See the flames feel the heat
Flying high, I am reborn.

Broken Hearts and Promises

Take a look around you baby
You can see what my heart needs
Everything about you lady,
Makes my soul feel free.

You have to know what I want now
You have to feel the heat
Babe I need your love and how.
Remember how we met.

Chorus:
It seems so long ago we shared
The words that made us one.
Now it seems you just don't care
As all we shared comes undone.
Broken hearts and promises.

See our little girl in pink
Spittin' image of her mom
Growin' up too fast I think
No more time to play and run.

Look how tall our boy has grown
Looks and acts just like his dad.
Wants to play guitar and show
The world how its been so bad.

Chorus:

Always Forward

Forward always forward
Eyes ahead and facing front
One foot in front of the other
Moving towards the future.

Forward always forward
Keep on trudging onwards
The daily grind continues on
Every moment draggin' down

Forward always forward
Open heart and open mind
Ready to receive and give
Not really sure if the path is right.

Forward always forward
Try and try again
I'm ready and willing to receive
Give me a sign it's worth it.

Forward always forward
Never give up hope
Heart yearning seeking love
Until at last there you were

Forward always foward
Towards the love we found
Fulfilling hearts desire
At last you're in my arms

Forward always forward
A future filled with support
A past that taught us much
Together we'll conquer fear

Forward always forward
My love has found a home
To share with you and receive
At last we have each other.

Give Me a Break

He ducked his head
Shuffled his feet
Blushing bright red
He whispered "you're sweet"

Chorus:
Give me a break
She said with a grin
I know you'll take
Even try to win
My heart and my soul.

His face lit up
A smile revealed
His hand it cupped
Her hand as he kneeled.

Run away with me
Walk under the stars
Our hearts can be
Wild and free afar

Chorus:

Today you've taken
My heart and soul
Now you're making
My heart overflow.

I'll run away with you
My heart was yours
If you'll always be true
I'll be forever yours.

Right There

You came into my life
Like a breath of fresh air
You promised me freedom
Somehow it seemed right
The way I gained a backbone
Made everything feel alright.

The memory of your scent
Lingers still in the air
The taste of your sweet lips
Caressing mine even though
You are not with me here.
My heart felt it was alright.

Chorus:
And then we were right there
We were in each other's arms
We tasted those sweet lips
And then we were right there.

The memory of your love
Reaching out in the middle
Of the night to hold you
The dreams that still continue
To haunt my waking moments
Asks if I'll be alright.

My aching broken heart
Can't remember how you felt
Even though it was just weeks ago
I can't picture those blue eyes
Without a tear rolling down
And I know you're not alright.

Chorus:

Now I'm moving on these days
My heart it's aching still
And I know that no matter what
My past will haunt me heavily.
I shed my tears over yours
Someday we'll both be alright.

When You Spoke My Name

How often do we pass by
Turn our head and miss
That look of wishing.
Our mind pre-occupied.

We need to be in tune
With the world around us
There are so many times
Missed connections happen.

When you spoke my name
Reached out with your soul
Connected to my heart
Reached into my future.

I've been standing there
So many times before
Probably spoken
Likely crossed your path.

This time it clicked between
Two souls seeking out
The connections right
Do you take that chance?

When you spoke my name
Reached out with your soul
Connected to my heart
Reached into our future

Coffee, tea and talking
Hashing old history
Sharing stories of the past
Speaking from the heart.

It couldn't be more plain
That it was meant to be
Scared to speak the truth
Embarrassed, blushing.

When you spoke my name
Reached out with your soul
Connected to my heart
Reaching into a future.

A Rainbow's Gift

Red was the color of His blood
Flowing from hands and feet
Nailed up on that cross
Crown of thorns upon his head
"Forgive them Father" he cried
What greater gift can we receive.

Orange were the tiger's stripes
The two of them pacing the deck
An old man's vision led them there
To follow all the other mammals
No enemies or prey to shred
Until the flood waters receded.

Yellow were the sands of time
That washed across the desert
Chasing that ragtag band
Following an old man's vision
From burning bush to mountaintop
Stone tablets to be believed.

Green were the locusts that rained
Down upon Egyptian cities
A plague of many brought to bear
Release my people He demanded
Set them free from slavery
Or more will die for your arrogance.

Blue was the river water
When that baby was set free
In a basket floating downstream
To be found by that queen
Raised as her own child
Later to challenge her son.

Indigo was the heavenly sky
When the star lit the night
For three kings to follow
From lands far away
To greet a newborn King
Sent from heaven to teach them.

Purple is the color of royalty
Yet no king of earthly design
Can offer the sanctuary and peace
Of living in the light of His love
Heavenly father we thank thee
For the gift of your only Son.

Happy Valentines Day

When she opens wide those eyes
Turns that gaze in his direction
All the world will disappear
And his soul is lost forever.

When his lips part in a smile
Whispered words of love
When he says her name
Her heart will melt again.

His heart will sing her praises
Her soul will fly so high
On this special day of love
She'll whisper those words too.

Happy Valentines Day my love
May this day be great for you.
Filled with happiness and joy
Across the miles or near by.

Heartaches

Another road trip
Travelling north
Driving alone
No radio
No country music
Just my own thoughts

Heartache and pain
Feelings of loss
Missing your scent
Missing my kids
How to explain
What can I say

Have to go on
Work is work
There is no choice
Each time the same
Never gets easier
Still feel the same

Heartache and pain
Still so alone
Sleep doesn't come
Lay there awake
My thoughts on you
My heart aching more

I miss my kids
As they grow up
I miss the times
I've not been there
I try to make up
Now that they're big

Heartaches mean love
I know each time
How much I feel
Never truly alone
Your words reassure
That we'll be alright

These are the things
I dwell on when
A road trip begins
Driving north again
Tears so close by
I bite my lip

Heartache and healing
Not all so bad
It means to me
That we can be more
Than just another
Statistic of theirs

So please believe me
These are not easy
For me to go do
I miss you too
Long distance bills
Don't mean a thing.

A Poet's Soul

Your teachers will tell you
That poetry must rhyme
You have to watch your syntax
Octets and septets and crap like that
They'll tell you it has to be just so
That's the way it's always been.

What they don't pass on to you in school
Is what the poet's really trying tosay
What else is he trying to convey?
A poet is not just putting words
Together for the fun of it.
He's passing on to you his darkest part.

A poet speaks with his soul
Bares his heart and exposes the dark
The lightest most romantic parts
Come out into the day to play
There is no deeper reason
Than to share that which cannot be jailed.

Don't be afraid to share your fears
Your loves and dreams and hopes
This is your space, your cave
The place you get to be yourself.
Give it all you've ever wanted
Spread the dark and the light.

Dreaming of Harley

If I had it my way I'd be riding
Sitting high up on a Harley
Riding winding backroads
Climbing hills and leaning low

Ain't nothin' better than the wind
Blowin' 'gainst your skin
Sun is shining down on you
Leathers gleaming dusty black.

I had myself a cruiser bike
Learning how to ride again
It wasn't the biggest one
But I was out there having fun

Loved leaning into corners
Getting as low and fast
As I could fly around
Sparks flashing off the pegs.

Laughing, grinning, howling
Life was good out on the road
My buddy Kevin up ahead
Slowing down to wave me on.

My dream was the Harley though
A newer truck did beckon me
Traded in my Kawasaki
Riding in a four wheel drive.

That Harley still beckons me
Calling out from Barnes I know
Denim black with plate laid back
Fatboy is it's name.

Maybe next year I say
Because I crossed it off the list
I had my motorcycle
Before I hit the big five oh.

I will ride a Harley soon I hope
Laughing again and having fun
Riding beside my friend
Wind and speed and sun.

Driving through the Valley

Headed out into the blue
Pale sky slowly lit up
Riding through the valley
She rode that beast of steel.

Winding backroads beckon
A day of wind and sun
Riding through the valley
She rode that beast of steel.

Nothing on her mind
Except loving every minute
Of riding through the valley
On that roaring beast of steel.

Stopped into see her brother
They rode more that afternoon
Riding up in the valley
Two riders on beasts of steel.

The afternoon was waning
Time to head on home to rest
No more in the valley
Westward on the beast of steel

Traffic was backed up forever
Headed eastward bound
An accident in the valley
Easy riding that beast of steel.

She never saw it coming
That beat up van it bolted
Trying to escape the valley
It smashed that beast of steel

Her body flying through the air
Please let the traffic miss me
I don't want to die in the valley
The beast of steel was done.

Four years later she remembers
The pain and firefighters
Rushing into the valley to
Save that rider of the beast of steel.

Brave cannot describe it
How she made it through that fight
I'd ride through the other valley
Beside her on a beast of steel.

Inner Voice

Open the door to your soul
Open the window to your heart
The universe is calling
Don't hesitate in seeking
The answer to your prayers.

The voice inside you knows
All the answers that you need
Have faith in your inner self
Know that you have the power
To choose the proper path.

This doesn't mean you have to rush
No need to jump both feet in
But keep an open mind about you
And trust your intuition.
That inner voice is speaking to you.

Heart and souls not broken
A universal truth alive
We CAN achieve full potential
Reach that greater plane
If we open our souls to truth.

Positive energies they flow
Through the cosmic web
Pulling on the strings of life
Allowing many lessons for us
As we walk the paths we choose.

Learn the lesson well
Heed the inner voice
Know when it is time
To spread your wings
Fly higher in the universe.

Welcome Home

Too many nights spent all alone
Too often waking up on the floor
No idea what went on the night before
How many times he's let his son down
Not showing up despite that call
Ex-wife asking where the hell are you
Now another job is on the line
He's got to get his shit together
Or he'll end up down on Main Street
Sleeping in the alleys and begging for food.
No way can he sink that low
He's a man of means, he's got pride
But pride is not enough to save
What's left of that man inside
She can't watch him crash and burn
Not going to let her son see what's left
Of the man she once loved so much.
Run away, run away and hide
Cover your eyes and plug your ears
Not going to listen to his screams
Why oh why did she leave he begs?
God why do you hate me so much.?
Bring back the love we once knew
I only want to be together again.
Let me show her the man I can be.
And another night finds him drunk
Passed out on the couch again.
This time he doesn't wake up
Pain of living without his family
Dragged his soul from hell to God
Who forgives him for all his sins.
Welcome home my child, love Me.

My Little Ones

When you look into the mirror
And you see me lookin' back
I know you'll remember
I did the best I could.

To be the kind of Daddy
That earned your trust and love.
It's not just a given fact
And it's not accepted truth.

Chorus:
But if you love yourself enough
Then you'll be able to admit.
That you deserve the very best
Because it's what I taught to you.
It's what I talked to you about
When you were growing up.

Be the best that you can be
No matter what the world says
There can be no greater love
Than your father has for you.

For you're a blessing in my life
And I count them every day
You are my son and daughter
And I love you both so much

Chorus:

It's not like everybody says it is
Not so easy as they make it look
On those big screen televisions.
Everybody sitting round the table.

But if you look into the mirror
And see me lookin' back
Then I know that you'll remember
How much I loved you both.
How very much I love you both
Every single day.

Howling Winds

The snow covered hills
Surround the valley
Slopes once green
With grape vines galore

The winter winds blow cold
Howling through window cracks
Heaters working overtime
To keep the chill at bay.

When all else fails
It’s time to hunker down
Pull the blankets up over
Cuddle up together beneath.

Not Enemies

I thought about the past
Looking through the lens of time
I wondered how I'd made it
Where did the time go I asked.
My hair is gone and beard is grey
There's wrinkles now beside my eyes
My babies are almost adults
One graduating, the other not far behind
My life has not gone as planned
The dreams I share with my best friend
All torn asunder by decisions wrong.
Dream house sold, marriage split
We fought like lions over meat
The kids were caught between us
Now finally we both can see
Though not friends, at least not enemies.

Circle of Life

I look out across the prairies
Winter bleakness all about
No sign of life in all the brown
Then a screech of victory sounds
A red-tailed hawk explodes
Out of the ground with fresh kill
Clutched in talons gleaming red
Reaffirming the circle of life.
Death for that mouse
Yet food for more than thought,
For the fledgling hawks.
Even when we cannot see it
Life continues all around us.

Beautiful BC

Trees flash by at roadside
Flying down that rural road
No time to stop and stare
Mother Nature's fresh white robe.
Economies must be grown
A job to do and then another.
How I'd love to stop with camera
To capture all that beauty
Jack Pines and larches
Boughs bent under the weight
A sigh escapes my lips
As another side road beckons
Come explore the back country
Of beautiful B.C.

Daddy

I've got a little girl
Who calls me Daddy
And a little boy
Who wants to be like me.
Yet I look into the mirror
And can't imagine why
I'm so freakin' far from flawless
I just don't understand it.

I just do the best I can
Tryin' to muddle through
Make sense of every feeling
That they are going through
Lend an ear or shoulder
Or wrap them in a Daddy's hug
To be the best darned Daddy
And not like the one I had.

Make or Break

There's a song on the radio
For all the feelings we have
Making up and breaking up
Falling in love and havin' babies
But there's no song written yet
For how I feel about you.

You made my heart leap high
Dance circles up in the sky
When we met I thought you were
My one and only girl.

Where do the feelings go?
How come the magic disappears
Why do your eyes fill with tears
Whenever I talk about my dreams.
We should have started over
Sought advice or counseling.

Now my heart is so low
Ashes of burnt desire
Only smoldering remains
Of a love that burned so brightly.

Hailey's Song

When you were just a little girl
I knew there was so much in store
For this life you were going to live
Would be the biggest adventure.

Can you imagine my surprise?
Now that you are eighteen years old
Practically a woman full grown
Yet so many ways my little girl

You've surprised me so many times
The thoughtfulness you've shown
How mature you seem to be
Yet call me to tattle on your bro.

Life out in the real world can be
Scary, frightening and yes sometimes
Even more than a little bad.
But you are strong and I trust you.

Don't be afraid, don't look back.
Never doubt and think what if.
You've got the best of both of us
You're my daughter and hers too.

Hailey you'll always be my baby girl
No matter how old you get
Or where you travel too.
You'll always be able to come back home.

My arms are always open as is my heart
There is no greater love for you
Than that which I have tried to show.
My daughter, my baby girl, I love you so.

Monsters

The closet door was slightly open
The darkness within complete
My bedside lamp had burned out
The night light was not enough
To dispel the fear of that within
The monstrous maw of dark.
The covers pulled up tight
To cover me completely
What they could not see
They might not grab
And drag within their lair.
I could hear their teeth a'gnashin'
O the stench of fetid breath
I had promised mom I'd not scream
Or ever wet the bed again.
But those fingers stretched from within
That darkened closet cave.
I closed my eyes and said a prayer.
"Please Lord deliver me from evil
I'm only five years old and scared."
My mouth it stretched wide open
I was just about to scream.
My bedroom door swung wide open
The hallway light beaming in.
A hero once again to me.
"Why little man what is going on,
How come it is so dark in here?
Let's dispel this darkness
I've brought you happiness
A light bulb colored blue
To ease your worried mind.
The colors of the ocean and
Of your momma's eyes.
No monster's fangs can touch you
Protected by this light.

It won't burn out or go dim
It's protected by your parent's love.
For you are my darling child
For whom I would gladly give
The moon and stars above
To keep you safe and warm at night.
Good night my little boy
Sleep tight wrapped in our loving light

Walking Forward, Looking Back

A river of red
Across the polished stone
Heavy scent of iron
Permeates the air.

Burgundy stain spreading
Like a glass of merlot
Spilled on a white carpet
Soft sighs like fall breezes.

Like a fish out of water
The edges gasp and pulse
The river slows then ends
Droplets ease to nothingness.

One last sigh escapes
Then silence creeps in
And fills the void
Like echoes across a silent pond.

A life extinguished
No more breathing in and out
By his own hand
It exists no more.

And that child's family
Will forever struggle
Walking forward, looking back
What more could have been done.

The note simply said
I can't take anymore
The bullies at school
Simply won't leave me alone.

I have no one to talk to
No one even cares
I'm sorry I've hurt you,
Mom and Dad I'll always love you.

Dysfunctional

The little boy
Closes his eyes
His eyes fill with tears.
He clutches his pillow
To his chest
And tries to plug his ears.

In the room next door
His sister sits
Turns up the radio
Head down on her desk
Homework stained with tears.

In unison they both think
Oh, how I wish they'd stop.

From down the stairs
The sound of shouting just gets worse.
Then finally as it always does
The front door slams
And Daddy's truck takes off.

Momma sits on the bottom step
Her anger plainly written
On her face.
The bills sit on the kitchen table
Empty wine bottle beside the sink.
She shakes her head
Anger and denial plainly etched
Across her stormy brow.

It's all his fault
She thinks
Just as she always does.

That young man
Sits behind the wheel of his pickup truck
Head in his hands against the wheel
He fights back the tears
Her handprint still glows red
Upon his cheek.
The echo of her words in his ears.

"I want a divorce.
I'm seeing someone else.
Get your stuff and leave.
You'll never see your kids again."

Picking up his cell phone
He makes the call as he always has
Ready to apologize
For what she blames him for,
Being such a loser.

A ragged sigh escapes
As the other end starts to ring.

Silence

Silence surrounds
Wrapped in it's cocoon
Quivering and weeping
Standing up
Breaking free
Laughing with relief
No need to fear
This is not the end
But a beginning
A new start
Ready to take the leap
Alone not lonely
A new home
A new life
Silent but not quiet
Peaceful and at peace
A heart not broken
But like the phoenix
Rising from the ashes
Born again to live
Free

Too Much / Not Enough

Moonlight keeps the wolves at bay
Sunlight keeps the crops to growin'
Night lights keep the monsters away
Halide lights keep the four-twenty goin'

Tungsten lights soon to be extinct
Small fluoro lights to keep us green
Black lights to party and dance in
Orange sodium lights to drive between

Moonlight reflects off dancing waters
Sunlight refracts through falling rain
Night light transforms clay for potters
Metal halide light as athletes train.

Incandescent light gives a healthy glow
Curly fluorescent lights with mercury poison
Black lights help the dealers with their blow
Sodium street lights expose drive by shootings.

Road Less Travelled

Fastidious and pretentious
Our words are merely that
How can we pretend to know
When we have only just begun.

The journey of a lifetime
One foot in front of the other
Work and life can drag you down
Yet a smile can lift you up.

Our world is changing rapidly
Technology supposedly saving us
Yet is it this or spirituality
That lights the fires in our souls.

So many signposts, omens if you will
Pointing a path less travelled
A road hidden within ourselves
We often traverse it alone, not lonely.

The light of heavenly love will guide
Through methods of our choosing
Prayers and hymns shared in a church
Meditation, yoga, tarot cards spread out.

The peace and love we can achieve
Then shared with one and others
To light the path no longer hidden
A road less travelled but worth the extra time.

Change Within

The winds of time call through the soul
Time for change and rebirth
Feel the heat searing away the past
New feelings and raw emotion
Trust the light, feel the greatness
There is no time like the now to reach
For the stars above reveal your love.

The sands of fate drop slowly down
The time-clock of life ticking away
Stuck in this moment of defeat
We feel helpless and beaten down
Blaming the past, searching for answers
Or looking too far ahead into the future.
Not able to grasp that now is the change.

Raindrops fall towards the earth
Looking up into the sky we're blinded
Water surrounding us from birth
Yet within it we gasp for breath
Without it we will die and wither.
From within it we are born into the air
To live within the light of the sun.

We reach toward the light with words
Spoken, sung, whispered and prayerful
O Lord we ask this in your name, we seek
The answers to so many prayers we beg
When He doesn't answer some may curse
As if He knows our hearts better than ourselves
His light will guide us forward higher than before.

Life in the Fast Lane

Faith is often hard to find
Flying down the road too fast
It's like we're losing our mind
Days are done, become the past
Too tired each night to love
Too busy each day to care
Don't even notice above
There's more to life than we dare.
Accepting there's a bigger
Picture to all that we're living
Doesn't see that he digs her
No matter how his heart sings.
Slow down and breathe deep, my heart
Is telling you don't depart.

The Great Wyrm

The dragon's breath plumed within the air
The knight's heavenly crest gleamed with gold
Green dragon poised to strike
Heavenly symbol, knotted cross
With a mighty crash they met,
Knight's protector, dragon's scale.
Back to back they stood against the world.

The Wyrms of Time

Picaro Ebano
Lays atop mounds of treasure
Dark evil cavern
Greatest wyrm of charcoal.

Master Malevolo sits
On throne of darkest midnight
Fingers tapping
Against his bearded chin.

Celestial Blanco
Dragon atop the mountain
Heavenly light
Greets the morn with a roar.

Mistress Cielo
Sits in the sunlit window
Smile spreads
Across her rose petal lips.

Lleno Verde
Soaks in the abundant spring
Emerald wings fan
The spring's heat surrounding.

Master Caudoloso
Swimming within the pool
Feet kicking
He caresses the dragon.

Armonia Zafiro
Soars through skies of azure
Blues blending
With peace and harmony.

Mistress Tranquilo
Astride the blue wyrm shoulders
Knees gripping
Eyes of chocolate full of soul.

Amado Rosado
Sets atop the castle parapet
Radiating love
Wyrm created by Nambi's design.

Mistress Amor
Stranger in a stranger land
Stands beside
Hand wrapped around dragon's talon.

These are
The great wyrms lost in the past
Time to tell
Their stories of bravery and love.

The Stag

And the game is afoot
Let there be no mistake
The prey has been sighted
The hunter's senses alert

The stag stands proudly
All majestic and glory
Outlined in the pre-dawn
Lifts his head challenge bugled

The hunter lifts his horn
To answer that challenge
There'll be no escaping
This time the prey will be his.

The stag sends his family
Away for their safety
This is one battle
That is his and his alone

The hunter continues
On through the dappled woods
With each clearing they pass
The signs point to victory

Then at last he is there
Just beyond decent shot
He's afraid that he'll bolt
Still a little bit closer

The stag's mighty rack
Blends in with the branches
The slightest breeze blowing
His nostrils flare with concern

The hunter steadies his aim
He'll only get this one shot
The sight lines are perfect
With a press of his finger

The camera starts clicking
The stag turns his head away
Then walks out of the trees
The pictures are perfect.

Gorgeous Green Eyes

She’s a tall drink of water
And she’s easy on the eyes
With legs that go up forever
Raven hair down past her shoulders
Eyes so green you’re lost in fields
Of wildflowers as sweet as her scent.

She’s looking for Mr. Wonderful
Searching for more than a friend
Hoping she’s going to find that spark
That’ll ignite a fire inside
Chemistry but not out of control

Betrayal

Anger and hurt
Swirl through his psyche
Betrayal so deep
It's felt to the soul.
Forgiveness
Can't even be
Imagined.

Why
Can't be answered
There are no reasons
Life goes on
No matter
How much the lies
Cut to the quick.

Family Settlements

What happens when you lose
Sight of what's important
How do you get up every morning
Where and when no longer matter.

Staying up late at night
Watching foreign films
Sleeping all day Saturday
Because you've nothing else to do

The family life you once shared
Surrounded by so many kids
The dirty diapers, runny noses
And yet together it all seemed to work.

I loved getting up so early
Making pancakes or waffles

Seeing faces light up
At the sight of blueberry sauce.

The simple things in life
Bring joy to each and every day
Waking up beside you
Falling asleep in your arms.

This used to be enough to live with
Settling seemed like all we had.
Now I'm on my own and looking back
I know that there is so much more ahead.

Sonia

Captured by those pools of chocolate
Enraptured by the petals of dark rose
Drowning in that dark satin sky.

PAIN ! ! !

The pain pulses periodically
Through, around, within.
He knows, feels, lives it.
POUNDING.

There is no surcease
How can he find relief
Nothing will ever help
despair.

Since he was very little
Head aching, brows pulsing
Explosions ripping into his brain
SCREAMS.

WHY ?
MAKE IT STOP !
God, I'll do anything
please ?!?

Darkness overtakes him
The soothing balm of drugs
Eases him into nether land
gone.

Not true relief for him at all
He knows the demon shall return
Not knowing what triggers it
Waits.

Anywhere, anytime
Falls down clawing at the sidewalk
Smashes his head into the wall
STOP!

Loving arms wrapped around him
Woman's voice begging him
Darling, lover, come back
easy.

And again, repeatedly
He knows there is only one way
To escape the fearsome devil
SHOT !

The note simply said I cannot
The shot had echoed throughout
The neighbours found him there
dead.

Pain, endless, ceaseless
Painless now forevermore
No one knew how to help.
free ?

My Life

It speaks volumes to me
When I can't even look in the mirror
The guilt and the tears
Cloud my vision too much
To see more than a blur.
For some the answer lies in the bottle,
For others they're snorting and smokin'
But for me the tears don't even
Start to wash away the pain.
I can't even begin to imagine
What I've done to your heart.
But I know that I'll never be able
To make it up to you again.
That wall that you've built
To keep me out
Just keeps getting higher and higher
The longer we aren't talking.
I don't know how I'll ever
Manage to scale such a castle
As the one that I built
When I spoke so brokenly
About how I was feeling.
Own your words and speak your truth
Mean nothing now that I opened my mouth
The intent was true, but the words were wrong.
How can I ever repair
All the damage I have done
Built that castle, dug the moat
I don't have a dragon or pegasus
To fly so high,
To recapture your heart.
I have no ideas any more
On how to find my way
Back to your heart.
The minotaur's maze is nothing

Compared to how lost I feel
Without you here in my arms.

World Stage

For all the world's a stage
The players circle round
When the world stops turning
Then the play will end
Until that happens
Then let us enjoy the ride
Live each day like it's our last
Contemplate your actions
Think about your words
Speak softly with a kind heart
And open doors that way
To a brighter future.

Hand in Hand

When I'm walking in the Light
Hand in hand side by side
Emerging from darkest night
Pushing hard against the tide

How many times we've walked this path
Twenty lifetimes maybe more
Will it be better than the past
A love and life we've shared before.

Now you're my whole world and life
Revolving around each other
Reconnecting without strife
The Light reflecting like a mirror.

The scent of your perfume wafts
Surrounding me and takes away
The stress of living each day fast
It's time to live within each day.

And once again the Light does shine
Bringing peace and joy to us
Live this life and be as mine
For my love this is more blessed.

Living in each moment's reward
Not giving in to life's demands
Love and laughter move us forward
Sharing, touching, hand in hand

Walk with me in the Light my love
Love with me side by side
Hand in hand, always in love
Always at each other's side.

Lifetimes

When I think about the past
I cannot help but wonder why
There were so many paths
That should have led to you.
What did I do without you
Why did it take so long?

It seems as though it's been
A lifetime maybe more
Since I held you in my arms

I remember the day I left
I knew I wasn't coming back
From the war that we were losing
You cried so many tears
I thought the gates of Heaven
Would be washed away.

It seems as though it's been
A lifetime maybe more
Since I held you in my arms.

Remember the time I was the one
Left behind to watch the ranch
We never knew that they were coming
The flames ate at the house so fast
You buried all of us beneath that tree
Out in that dry and barren ground.

It seems as though it's been
A lifetime maybe more
Since you held me in your arms.

So many times we've walked together
Shared love and shared a bed.

So many times we were denied
Unrequited love and lonely souls.
Lets make this one count my love
Give it everything that we have now.

It seems as though it's been
A lifetime maybe more
Since you held me in your arms.

I cannot remember all the past lives
They all start to blur together
If I suddenly remember then
It's snatched away and tampered with
By the Light who wants each time
To be a lesson learned not repeated.

It seems as though it's been
A lifetime maybe more
Since we were in each other's arms.

Time with You

There are times
When I lie awake
Dreaming of you

There are days
When I wish for more
Time alone with you

There are minutes
When I want to stretch
Them out to forever

There are hours
When I can't remember
Life before meeting you

There are seconds
When I blink and know
You are always with me

These are the times
The minutes, the seconds
The hours, I love you always.

Wicked

something wicked this way comes
weaving through the universe
stalking, spying, ever onward
something wicked this way comes

when it happens be prepared
the universe is watching you
seeking answers are you ready
the question on every tongue

wicked, cool, and happening
the soul opens to receive
the past is slipping away
healing, no more hurting, seeking

answers questions painful sharing
talking listening searching forward
review the past and share the pain
this way moving forward can begin

Burned

Burned once
Not gonna try
Lonely silence
Hearts desire

Online dating
No time for bars
Anticipating
Healing scars

And then we met
Hearts torn apart
Already set
Healing time starts

Joy

Bring joy to each day
Share a smile
Reach out and touch
Hold hands with someone special
Kiss often
Hug those who are comfortable with it
Offer hugs to those who might be
Smile at everyone it can brighten their day
Open doors for people
Breathe deeply and
Stay calm in moments of crisis
This too shall pass.
Give all that you can then a bit more
For in this way, you'll stretch yourself.
When it seems like too much
Reach out for a friend
A better understanding comes from sharing burdens
Live like each day was your last.
Share thoughts, share love, share food.
And in all matters be honest with yourself
It matters not what others think of you
Though we want them to think highly of us
That is not the most important thing
No, what is important is being true to your beliefs.
Knowing that you have done all that you can
To give of oneself when all else is unavailable
That is all you can do.
Strive for the higher state of consciousness
That comes from meditation and being still
For in this way, the universe can send the answers you need
Open your heart for love and beauty.
It is all around you, even in the smallest child
And the largest mountain
Love.

Unlock The Door

Country songs on the radio
Music turned way down low
Hear your voice it brings a smile
Calling out across the miles
Though we're far apart now girl
I'm on my way to our new world.

Driving through the long night
I just can't wait to be at your side
Been searching for your true heart
A lot of mis-steps on my part
Trying to find that connected soul
It's all that will make me whole.

Chorus:
Two hearts so true and light
Connected through eons of night
Found each other at last
Reconnecting from the past

The goddess in your soul
Pulls my heart strings close
That inner voice tells the truth
We were lovers on a distant path
Hold me close and never leave
Once again we're here, believe

People shake their heads my love
Not understanding how powerful
Past lives affect our current state
Righting wrongs and past mistakes
Love and then love some more
We've got the keys unlock that door.

Chorus:

The Cowboy and the Lady

The cowboy and the lady
Met beneath the full moon
On a hillside outside of town
He pulled her into his arms
Holding her in a hug he whispered
Lady run away with me
Be my lover and my wife.

She pulled away and looking up
She cried a tear or two and then
The lady asked the cowboy
Just hold me close and whisper
How much you love me dear
For I can't run away with you
There's still so much to do.

The cowboy wrapped his strong arms
Around the lady and whispered
My darling I'll wait for you
I'll wait and sing songs for you
Under the light of this full moon.
My lady love, I love you so
Someday, you'll run away with me
And we'll live together forevermore.

The lady sighed and leaned back
Against the cowboy's chest
She closed her eyes and sang to him
Of the love that she felt inside
How much her heart had hurt
How long she had searched
Giving up against all hope
Of ever finding the love of her life.

That cowboy and the lady
Ride across the sky together
He's waiting on the hillside
A full moon gazing down
She rides across the sky
Shining brightly lighting up the day
He waits at night reflecting her light
From across the other side

The Old Man

He stood there outside the liquor store
Head bowed down, cup held out
His feet wrapped in old towels
His pants all dirty, ripped and torn
His face was unshaven, several months.
The large hands were battered and shaking
His faded blue eyes rheumy with age
And many years of alcohol abuse.
That little boy walked over from
His mother's side and reached out
"Mister are you sad, you're crying?"
That old man slowly knelt down
Took the little boy's hands in his
That mother gasped and rushed over
And heard that old man whisper
"Son, you're the first one who came over
To see if I was alright today.
For that I'm going to give you
A very special gift.

That old man stood up tall and proud
The years flowed from him like water
Shedding off a duck's back
The little boy never even blinked
Though his mother tried to grasp his hand
And pull him to "safety and out of harm's way"
Foolish woman can't you see
This is the Savior sent here to free
Humanity from their chains and bonds
Put upon us by technology and devil's hands
The old man was no longer an old man
He stood there with an inner light
Shining proudly he turned to that boy
Kneeling down once more he whispered
"For you are my child, my son reborn

As it was before it is again,
Let the world rejoice and praise my name
Humanity deserves a second chance."
The old man hugged the child to his chest
Then releasing him he kissed his head

I have loved all of you so long
I had forgotten how much you've changed
My Name is no longer special
No one sings those psalms or hymns.
And yet this child chose to care.
God loves you all as do I
We ask nothing more than love returned
Heavenly Father, they do still care
I see it in their face and hearts.
No flood is needed, no pillars of salt
Just a small reminder from the heavens
An angel or a miracle to show them all
Of Our Love for all of them
No matter what their color, creed or temple.

Lights Across BC

Living in the northern parts
Up in Fort St John
The flatness of the prairie
Summer lights the nights

Living at the joining of
Fraser and Thompson
Rivers, mighty rapids show
Rainbows neon lights

Living in Vancouver's lights
Ocean, mountain play
Westcoast chill, relaxing with
Hollywood North stars.

No matter where you set down
Your roots to live here
BC is the place to grow
And find your future.

Canada a nation great
Has so much to share
None can surpass our Spirit
Shines in all we do.

Heaven's Gate

I remember as a child
How my cousins seemed so big
I thought that I could never be
As adult as they were.
But months to years passed by
Until one tragic day
My mother sat there crying
The phone just hanging down
Three cousins dead and now
They'll never know how much
I've grown to catch up.

My cousin Richard
Named after his father the railroad man
A wild crazy teen who thought
A couple drinks wouldn't hurt
After all it wasn't that
Which killed his pa
But that falling rock instead.
Those few drinks, a couple more
Then behind the wheel they got.
Driving home inebriated
But they were having fun.

The car swerved off the road
Upside down it lay within the ditch
Those deep water filled ones
In the lowlands of Richmond.
A son, a brother, a cousin
Gone because of drink.

That same year another cousin
Michael was his name.
On a motorcycle driving home
Rainy nights and once again

A drink or two of alcohol
The motorcycle slipped out from under
As they flew off of the pier
The wharves in Richmond claimed another
They found his body the next day
Floating in the inlet
Another son, brother, cousin dear
Claimed by alcohol.

Vacation in my dreams

Sundrenched beaches beckon me
Calling out across the sea
It's where I want to be
It's where I want to be.

Bleached white sand
Sun kissed skin getting tanned
It's what I want to do
It's what I want to do.

Cold icy drinks to imbibe
Never need to go inside
That's where I am
It's where I am today.

Cool it Cowboy

Looking back over years of memories
Always makes me double take
Could've should've running freely
Wonderin' if it would've made
A difference if I'd stayed.

Son and daughter on their own
Mothers workin' hard to avoid
Daddy calling on the phone
Want to see my kids
Access granted but ignored.

Judge says cool it cowboy
Momma needs to take a break
Kids are cryin, Daddy's trying
That boy needs his father
Daughter needs a daddy too.

The years pass by even though
Mom and Dad no matter what
Cannot agree, can't get along
And then a miracle occurs.

Beauty and the Beast

Walking through the mall
My head wrapped in clouds
Troubles they did surround
Circling pain and hurt.

What could I do or say
My world was crashing down.
And yet lost deep in thought
Only I can make it change.

The beast within me roared
The heavens opened wide
Tired of the rhythm of the rain
Sunshine shining through.

There she stood a smilin'
Face lit with an inner light
Advice was freely given
Offer of friendship accepted.

The beauty within her shone
I was dazzled and enraptured
And within that magic moment
My world was changed forever.

Pain it could not hurt me
The past was left behind.
No longer wrapped about me
I was moving down the road.

Rick Tippe sang the song
That yesterday is history
Tomorrow is a mystery
Today is a gift and that I accept.

For the present is meant for living
Life of beauty, no more beast
Let me walk beside you
Hold my hand and comfort me.

A Princess in Pink

I dated a woman who had two daughters
One wild and crazy, ready to party
The other young lady was so into pink
She painted her bedroom the color
Of Pepto Bismol.
I called her my princess
She called me her cowboy Dad
No greater gift could be given
Than to be trusted like that.
And though her mother and I
Didn't last very long
The bond between that princess
And her cowboy dad
Remains just as strong as the first day
When we met in her driveway.
Don't ask me why or how
I don't need to explain to you or another
Just as long as you know that the love
That we share
Is pure as any parent can feel
For a child of his own.
Ashley is my little princess in pink
Always was and always will be.

Meant to Be

My soul is floating freely
Whispers through the air
What am I meant to be?

I feel alive, yet missing
Something inside feels lost
What am I meant to be?

My mind is sharp, alert
Penetrating deep inside my heart
What am I meant to be?

My life it fell apart
Not once, but twice
What am I meant to be?

And still my soul survives
Fighting on stronger than before
What am I meant to be?

I'm a survivor, fighter
Life is meant to be more than this
What am I meant to be?

My spirit soars on wings
Borne aloft with creation
What am I meant to be?

I have the eyes of the poet
Soulful, loving, seeking more
What am I meant to be?

I am alive for a reason
Still yet to be determined
What am I meant to be?

Loving my children
Being the dad I want to be.
This I was meant to be!

Being an electrician
All that I was trained to be.
This I love to be.

There is one thing more I need
To share a soul connection
This I will someday be.

Holding On and Letting Go

Reaching out for something
I never really knew
How much my leaving
Was going to hurt you.

It's been said so many times
The hurt it has built up
Both of us just wanting
A more than half full cup.

And still my heart is yearnin'
And still my soul it aches
Even though we know it's over
How much hurtin' can it take.
When we're only holding on
And it's time for letting go.
Letting go.......

Seeking Light

When you're surrounded by the sharks
Treading water and asking why
Instead of seeking answers
To questions that have no answers
Instead request from that greater good
To bring you answers that you need
Living in the moment
And seeking only the light and good
Can change the outcome of many
Maybe if we focus on the positive
Ask for all that we need
That is what we will receive

Road Trip

Leaving in the morning
Headed up the highway
Sky is black and raining
You know further north is snow.

Headed into those black clouds
The job is calling me
Can't avoid this drive now
Six inches of snow on the road.

Following the snow plow
Up the long hill to the snow shed
Semi trucks jackknifed everywhere
Three cars upside down.

It was scary driving and I called
But hung up the phone
When the car swerved to much
Wanted you to know I cared.

Made it up there in four and a half
Hours longest drive ever
My arms they hurt from holdin' on
White knuckling all the way.

One hour to do the job
Turn around head back home
Dinner at Samuel Robertson
Looking around to check it out.

Who I Am

I'm perfectly fine,
With my hairline
It's headed north
But then of course
I happen to like
A heartfelt cry
When I'm at the show.
Oh Baby........
You oughta know
That I'm perfectly fine
With who I am..........

I don't need to fool.........
Around on you
No need to look
At those kinds of books.
You're more than enough
To break through this tough
Shell that surrounds
My heart since it's found
You.........

You might want to think
I'm gonna sing
This little tune
About somebody new
As matter of fact
You're on the right track
The person I've found
Is just me, myself.

(spoken)
Now wait a minute......

Just what did you mean
I really can't see
What foolin' is this?
It makes no sense
Oh Baby.........
I'm happy enough
With who I am.............

"journey" **a SLAM poem**

i am a creator
one who loves to make things
give me a pen and paper
i'll be happy for hours writing
i cannot draw a picture
i cannot paint or sketch
but with my words i'll paint
pictures that will rock your world
soaring up to heaven
sinking down to hell
majestic mountains and prairies flat
i'll show you the world around
her strawberry hair or hazel eyes
my daughter has hair of honey
my son has muscles bulging
take a trip through inner space
hear about the Light or love
walk with me through the world
i'll show you what i see and hear
follow on this journey
or lead me along as well
i can walk beside you
or carry you when needed
we are all brothers in this land
meant to reach out helping hands
love, what can i say, it has been
a journey of ups and downs
but then so it goes for many
we love, we fight, we move
we fall apart sometimes
for no reason at all
not settling, not giving in
no more time to lose our souls
sucked dry by inattention
or made so small by derision

what started out as one tiny
pinprick
has ballooned into a fiery hell
that consumes you night and day
lashing out you leave
then come crawling back
you ask, you plead,
you beg
it begins all over again
oh this journey is not yet over
yet we turn to another page
the kids are almost adults
moving on
growing up and trying so hard
to be independent
you want to hold them
hug them
kiss them
tell them it will all be great
sometimes they trip and fall
or stumble
but they are strong
you've raised them well
they know how to get on with it
and still
if you could you would
you know you would
you wish
don't you
that you could
turn back time and hold them once more
as babies
tuck them in and read them stories
just one more time
this is a good time
but
still

you would if you could, one time
friends
they are many
yet so far away
so close with this web
struggling through
just like us all
standing tall and humble
writers, painters, artists, sculptors
family too here abide
a sister, brother, cousin
father figure better than dad
mother if i could
thank god it's not "my" mom
too sane not crazy like my own
supportive, reaching out
backing off, yet still close by
ready always
i love you
hugs
prayers
like blood
flowing
veins pulsing
life giving
friends
young and old
a princess
so many stars
heart to heart
knowing when to say
and when to just hold
and say nothing
i would give you anything
because i know you would too
we never talk about our exes here
somehow it just seemed wrong

but would we be here
in this place
this space
without them
for in their own way
they too have helped us grow
i think sometimes
they have a special place
oh we have those strong feelings
anger
sometimes even hate
and yet deep inside
where we let no one see
there is some small kernel
seed
that says in tiny writing
i still love some part of you
there were times
good times amongst the bad
waxing philosophical
it might be the snow
or the fact that life
has not been easy
oh i know it's not hard
not like i live in haiti
or new zealand
earthquake ravaged
disease spreading
looting, raping, killing
no, i live here in bc
beautiful bc they say
yet no better than say
pennsylvania or new york
its all the same really
we eat, sleep, work, play
we talk, we walk, and then
do it all again

for what
why
i suppose we're searching
for that one
that spark
chemistry
soul ....
connection
yet is there really only one
is not each time a step
towards
perfection
that final love
we find with
Light
we need the love
of another
here on earth
it reminds us
that we will someday be
in the Light
of pure Love
but until then
go forth and seek
give
trust
open
love
live and never ever ever
give up

because i love you
you know i do

Imagine My Surprise

I never imagined
A life like this
Thought when I was older
I would be living in bliss.

I was sure surprised
After my best friend
Betrayed that trust
First marriage did end.

Not getting the advice
Needed to heal
My soul searching
Needing more

A second chance
Blond turned redhead
A blended family
Too much baggage

I never imagined
That life would change
Once again searching
Still needing answers

What will it take
How much can I handle
Is there no end in sight
To this feeling of loss

Sighs escape when
Life gets too much
I open my heart to the Light
Let God's love shine in

It helps to share
The burden of life
But it's me who has to
Pay the bills, not Him

Freedom of choice
Choosing my kids
Over a large house
And a family too

My kids lift me up
Their love and affection
Make each day easier
Knowing it's for them

That and still looking
For that spark and chemistry
That soul connection
She's out there I know

Imagine my surprise
When sitting across the room
I spied a redhead
Who caught my fancy

Could this be the one
To make me feel whole
To help me move forward
Beginning again

Imagine my surprise
First kisses
A little chemistry
It might be, we'll see

One day at a time
Imagination
Surprise
Chemistry and sparks.

Cowboy

Wearin' down his boot heels
Walking along the backtrails
Lookin' for those lost souls
Headed out 'long the fence rail.

Giddy-up and ki-yi-yay
That cowboy's song is real
Those little brown dogies strayed
Their mama's pain he feels.

There in the bush he sees a flash
Brown and white blendin' in
Quietly before it dashes
His rope he twirls just once.

Gentle hands reelin' in
Lead the calf back home
Carryin' that little one
Repeating his cowboy song.

Giddy-up and ki-yi-yay
Get along little dogies
Your mama is waiting
And we've got to go home.

Climbs back up in his saddle
Rope coiled back on his belt
The cook has hot coffee
The ice in his fingers to melt

His mama wanted him corporate
His pa thought he'd go trades
Followed his heart to the range
A ramblin' man he remains.

Exercising Demons

When he was just a little boy
His mother used to tell him son
This is going to hurt me more
Than you.

The wooden spoon on his backside
Left a mark deeper than the flesh
Haven't talked to her in years now
Can't.

History repeats itself
Watching younger mothers spanking
Reaching out to stop the pain
Hugs.

Why do they resort to violence
Can't they feel that child's pain
See the expression on their faces
Hurt.

Being wrapped in loving arms
Kisses and sweet whispered words
No greater reward than little arms
Returned.

give
love
hug
kiss
take
away
pain
don't
cause
more

Sweet little child of their youth
Remember only that which hurts
No memories of happiness
Pain.

Screaming, running, hiding away
No mommy, no no no stop
I won't do it anymore, no
Screams.

Have to stop the cycle of hurt
Not repeat the same mistakes
I love you baby child of mine
Peace.

Love = Peace
Hugs = Joy
Rewards = Good memories

Light

We come into this earth
From darkness.
We open our eyes
To the light.

We close our eyes
It is so bright.
We wander through
The night
That comprises
Our life.
Searching for light.

We grope
Our way through each day.
To the light.
At the end of our lives
We walk
Towards the light.

Our days are filled with
Longing.
Our nights are sweetened
By the light.

Imperfections abound
We seek.
The perfection of the light.
Peaceful.
Calmness and love fulfilled
With light.

Colton's Song

My little boy ain't little no more.
He's almost a man no longer a child.
He's in between and wanting so bad.
He's trying to find his place in the world

He's my son
In more ways than one.
And I want him to know
I'm always trying to show
That I am so proud
Of the man he's becoming.

That's my little girl and she'll always be mine.
No matter where she ends up going.
She's always welcome to hugs and kisses
When she catches sight of those butterflies.

She's my daughter
In more ways than one
I want her to know
I'm always trying to show
That I am so proud
Of the woman she's become.

Fight

Someday I'll sit there with my kids
Tell the story of how I fought for them
They might not understand it now
But I know that in their hearts
They will know how much my love for them
Made me struggle day and night.

Love that little girl full of smiles
Hug that little boy full of giggles
Hold them close to my heart
Watching them grow up so fast
Sorry that I couldn't be there
Daddy's love will have to suffice

Their mother and I fought a lot
But they don't remember that
All they can hear are the good times
Which is they way it should be
For children don't need to know
The pain that two adults can afflict.

Fighting never solves at thing
We'd be better off to walk away
The mental stress of dealing with
Everyday life is more than enough
Supportive partners needed more
Than the daily battle couples endure.

We fought in court and in email
We argued constantly once I met
Another lady who said why do you
Let her tell you what to do and when
These are YOUR kids, stand up for them
My ex saw it another way, interference.

I'm on my own but not for long
My heart is empty and needs a home
Someone who will stand by my side
But not shadow me or make me hide
No longer need to fight with the ex
Won't fight with someone who'll cherish me.

Someday

Someday, someone will walk into your life
And you will realize in that moment
Why it never worked with anyone else.
The glance across the room will capture
More than just your heart.
Your soul will feel the fire
You will know it deep inside.
It doesn't have to be a raging fire
No fireworks exploding overhead
Just that bit of chemistry
That spark that lets you know
That first kiss that leads to more
The look in her eyes just enjoying you
Being there at her side.
Your hand on her back or on her knee
The fingers you feel entwined with yours.
Her breath on your chest
As you watch TV with each other
Her head resting against you.
Being the cheerleader to her music
Having her support for your writing.
Knowing that it's a perfect fit
The life you've always dreamed
Was just out of your grasp.
Someday this will all come true
So keep the faith, believe in you.
There is a day that the world will stop

And there she'll be in front of you
All the time you wasted online dating
The ones who led you astray
With stories that were simply not true.
It's time that someday came about
That someday could be today.

LOVE

This is not the end of the journey
But merely the middle of the story
The part you try to skim through
To reach the end of that book
And find out if they lived happily ever after
But life isn't like a fairytale
There isn't always a prince or princess
Yet we keep on looking for that special someone
Who can make us feel that chemistry.
Don't give up hope
They're out there, somewhere
Over the rainbow, in the next valley
Hidden away behind a forest glen
No fairy dust or butterfly kisses
Can keep true love apart forever
Hope, pray, love, truth and beauty
Are just rewards for your patience.

Now and Then

I pass him in the underground parking
Every other day or so
An older man, grey hair, wrinkled
We nod, sometimes say hello
I wonder where he's going
Where is he coming from?
Looks too old to be working still
Shouldn't he be retired now?
What happened in his life?
That he has to carry on this way
Why isn't he down in Phoenix?
Golfing or sightseeing somewhere
Could that be my fate?
What if I end up like that?
Not saved enough or pensions gone
Who's going to take care of me?
When I'm too old to keep on
Keeping on?
Sure I'd like to travel the world
Stop in New York City
And visit an old friend or two
Head off to South Africa
Visit a wildlife refuge
Or swing on down through Utah
And see the oil rigs in Texas.
What if what I see in that old man
Is the future that's in store for me.
Should I do without right now
Stop living in the moment.
Save up every penny I make
Put it all away in retirement funds
A different what if plagues me though
What if I don't make it that far
Saved up all my dimes and nickels
To have a heart attack or even

Get in an accident.
Sure my kids will get the funds
It's not like it will be wasted
But the here and now must mean more
Than just a struggle to save for later
I don't want to hit eighty and think I wish
I could have had a motorcycle
I might have had me a tattoo
Could it be that there is a balance?
Between the now and then
I wish, I want, I have, I did without.
Somewhere in between all that
Is where I need to live
Not because an ex girlfriend told me so
Not because an ex wife wanted more
No, the here and now is a lesson
To be given to the future
So that my own two children
Can have some now and some later
They can watch how daddy balanced life
And made it all come together.
It wasn't easy, it never is
But if the balance of life is good
Then the memories of their youth
Will be too.

Simply Complicated – Duet

As I sat there on his couch
And I leaned back in his arms
I really like to feel your touch
Makes me feel so safe from harm
There's one thing you need to know

I'm a complicated woman
And I just might be a challenge
But I hope you'll be the man
Who can tame this wild heart

I reached forward stroked her hair
Leaned in and kissed her cheek
I'm not going anywhere
This cowboy's heart ain't weak
There's one thing I need to say

I'm just a simple cowboy
But I'm up for any challenge
Maybe you're the woman
Who can make me settle down

And now we've found each other
And we've healed each other's soul
Never need another lover
No more hearts out in the cold
There's just one thing left to sing

It's simply complicated
And we're both up for the challenge
When a woman loves her cowboy
And a cowboy loves his sweetheart
It's simply complicated
They're both up for the challenge
Yes it's simply complicated

Broken Hearts

How do you heal a broken heart
Where do you find the words
How does it feel to be whole again
When do you know it's time
To let go of that pain inside.

When she calls late at night
Crying how much it hurts
You want to hold her
Keep her safe in your arms
But you know that it's too late

How do you heal her broken heart
Where do you find the words
That will help her feel whole again
Why does it take so long
To let go of that pain inside

When you're laying there in bed
All alone with just your thoughts
And the only way out is the wine
To drink yourself to sleep again

How do you heal your broken heart
How many times have you walked away
To return to her side no questions asked
Why she asks is it different this time
Can't let go of that hurt inside.

And the text messages continue
Begging and pleading with you
Don't walk away from me
Don't make me face this alone.

How do you heal a broken heart
The strength to be strong inside
To stand up for yourself for once
The self esteem you need to move on.

And you know that someday
You'll both feel whole again
But the phone calls filled with crying
Still break your heart anyways.

Heavenly Reunion

And there it was in front of us
What could we do but stare
There was no way out of there
It just stood there like a yellow bus

One of us stepped forward
I don't remember who
Tapped against the side, halloooo?
No answer was coming, no word.

With a sigh, we turned around
Headed back to where we were from
Someone suggested coming with a gun
Instead we headed back to the ground

Heaven's gates were locked for us
The sun stood in our way
Tomorrow would be another day
I don't want to, one lady fussed

Always agony after awesome rise
One of the angels quipped
A soldier loosened his gun clip
Everyone else edged away from the guy.

Calmly, calmly called conductors
Don't you dare do dirty deeds
You're on the heavenly steeds
You'll be sent to drive tractors

Down in that demon's hell
Where city folk get sent
For paving over with pavement
Instead of leaving ground to till.

Like the dust bowls of the thirties
You'll toil under blazing suns
While all around you swirls tons
Of dust and dirt and demons nasty.

Why do we have to wait again
Why is Saint Peter not at his post
The angel's eyebrows rose
Where do you think he is my friend

He's attending to God's will today
Bringing home a special child
One who suffered for a little while
Wheelchair bound, couldn't play.

That child is more important to Him
Than the CEO and cheating housewife
For that child was loved his whole life
By a mother's love without end.

And with God's grace they will be
Together again within His light
Oh how she'll rejoice at the sight
When her son walks to her freely.

That housewife hung her head in shame
The CEO had tears in his eyes
They knew that they could abide
In purgatory's purging flame.

To all those who strode with me
To the pearly gates that day
Not one begrudged the delay
To allow the reunion of that family.

Something About a Rainstorm

I walk these dark and rain swept streets
Dancing 'tween the raindrops
Two steppin' like I've got two left feet
There's a love song makin' me feel lost

No lyrics left to carry that soulless tune
I've forgotten the words so many times
No more walks beneath that full moon
No more time for alibis and rhymes

Chorus:
'Cause the minute that I walked out
I knew there was no lookin' back
Doesn't stop me from rememberin'
The times we used to have our scraps
And there's somethin' about a rainstorm
That makes the memories full of pain.

I'm headed out the highway
For a show in one more town
There's no reason left for me to stay
On this steel horse I'm feeling down.

'Nother place where I'll try to forget
All the love we thought we'd share
'Cause there's something I don't get
How we let love just disappear.

‘Cause the minute that I walked out
I knew there was no lookin’ back
Doesn’t stop me from think’n ‘bout
When you threw your diamond at......me
Across the bed we had shared.
And there’s somethin’ ‘bout this rainstorm
That’s causing me so much pain.

Don’t know if I’ll return to sing
Can’t stand the thought of seein’ you
Dancin’ ‘cross the floor with him
But this steel horse remembers too.

How it felt with your arms ‘round me
Riding from town to town at night
And I know when the songs complete
I’ll be ridin’ on to sing one more night.

‘Cause the minute that I walked out
I knew there was no lookin’ back
Doesn’t seem easier without
You riding, coverin' my back.

And there’s somethin’ ‘bout this rainstorm
It’s causin’ me so much pain
Rememberin’ all the times we shared
Both the good times and the bad

Somethin’ bout the cold wet rain
Beating down on me that hurts so bad
‘Cause there’s somethin’ ‘bout this rainstorm
Making me feel awful down

Stabbed in the Back

The look in his eyes
Pain, hurt and disbelief
How could she
Why would she
What was she thinking
There were no answers
An empty apology
Just couldn't repair
The knife wound so deep
In his back.
Oh the way she cried
Was certainly real
No alligator tears
But it would never be
Enough to fix
His broken heart
He had opened his soul
Allowed her back in
He had already adjusted
Was used to the empty
Feeling of loss
Never should have
How could she
Why would she
Stab him like that
There wasn't really
An answer
Just more excuses

The Light in Your Eyes

Look in the mirror
See the light reflect
That's not just the fixture
It's so much more.
That is the Light of God's love
Shining in your eyes
Reflecting back at you.
Give thanks to Him
For giving you this day.
Let it be known
That you welcome Him
Into your life and heart.

Look up at the sky
See the light shine down.
That's not just the sun
But so much more.
That is the Light
Of His pure heart
Showering you with love.
Giving you the room
To grow into you.
So you can share
His love with the world.

Look at your children
See the light in their eyes.
That's not just their love
For you and life.
But His love coming through
Because you have shown
Their little hearts they're loved.
Not only by you
But from Him up above.

Sally

Strawberry blonde and hazel eyes
Smiling while her voice is singing
Incredible.
Watch her move across the floor
She can dance, love those moves.
Yowza.
Watching her across the dance floor
See her catch my eye and hope
Smilin'
Two more Thursdays had to pass by
Before she brought that birthday cake
Introduction.
Said goodnight, it was nice to meet you
Chuckled to myself walking out the door
Hooked.
Nervously asking Rocco about her
Did she say anymore to you?
Too young.
Yet there she was on the following week
Waiting to see if I was there too.
Lovely.
With her adopted moms she was at the Ranch
The three of them waiting there for me.
Relief.
Can you imagine where this was going
Not me, one day at a time this round.
Slowly.
And yet who are we to tell our soul
When and how to feel for another
Loving.
So welcome to my world Miss Sally
I hope that you will enjoy the ride
Me too.

World and Heavens

When the sun rises over the mountains
And the stars flee from the sky
I will be beside you through the day.
When the sun sets and dusk seeps in
The moon will rise and shine on you
I will be beside you through the night.
You are the world and I am the heavens
Let me revolve around you
I will be by your side both day and night
I would be your shadow and the light.
Let the wind howl around us
I will be your shelter and your home.
Let the snow and rain come down
I would be the one to cover you
With my warmth there would be no need
To ever be in fear of life's trials.
I will carry your burdens when you tire
And be there to listen to your stories.
There will be no word too small or loud
That I will ever turn away from.
For the world and the heavens
Will never part company just as I
Will always be at your side.

The Dark by Colton Robinsmith

They all try to stand out and be different,
But when we are all so used to it,
All we can see are lights in the dark,
No one cares about your shiny lights or flashy highlights,
I'm tired of putting up with all this heartache and blood hate,
When we are kids we believe in anything,
Now we are older and have lost faith in everything,
Open your eyes, we are the world, now we can be heard,
If not from a position of success then we are blessed,
With visions of the future not money but the life we live and the love we give,
Our lives are not measured on what you do when you're alive,
No, they are measured in the moments you live and what you leave behind,
And when it's so easy to suffer a loss of faith,
Stand up and take a shave and rid yourself of those who hate,
If you don't start believing in yourself sometime,
Then you say you don't want to feel this fame,
The fame that comes from being able to say things like someday,
So I say to you empathetically believe in yourself and all those around you,
Because if you don't know that I will, I will say to you someday,
Then you will believe just like me thorough and true,
Don't accept any less than you deserve take yourself to a new level of pure,
So sure why not expect it to be as good as you could,
But not on the same task rather give them your flask,
Not of water but your belief your motivation so someday we'll rule the nation,

No, not through government and all that spiteful judgment,
Or through war or militia don't try to rule me with your great big flotilla,
Maybe worse the threat of peace because there's nothing worse than to lose the best,

Petty Problems by Colton Robinsmith

And as the gods struck down upon us, they spoke to us,
They did not say for you to gloat, or even hope,
They did not tell us to survive, and abundantly thrive,
They didn't say for us to help those who can't help themselves,
They didn't say to shoot the painfully dying whelps,
They commanded us to find immortality and the ultimate sense of security,
They said we should forget the others, but why,
We have found immortality and the ultimate sense of security,
So why shouldn't we go further and beyond what we can achieve,
Instead of looking at the face of a dead man and leave,
We can find peace, it not in one of us it's in all of us,
So forget your petty problems, and your faceless demons,
If you died tomorrow what would you remember that would make you happy,
But rather instead and when you know you've achieved something,
You'll remember what made others happy,
Then only then will you understand that you were not meant to be king,
King of anyone or anything, we are all the jacks queens and kings,
The jokers the jesters, so remember this before you go trying to pester,
Me or anyone because if you think you have problems, you do,
There is something wrong with you, there are people with no shirt or shoe to their name,
And all you can do is complain, and yet you can't find shame,

In this, in anything you do, you're a blind fool,
Pretending to be a wise man, in my land, although in your land,
You are known to dance in front of bulls, now you just gotta know your going to be full of holes,

Depth perception by Colton Robinsmith

We have built from the ground up our civilization,
And we call it civilization yet its only in our nation,
No one sees the pain and suffering that everyone else goes through,
Let alone the pain and suffering in our own backyard,
Play and be different then its work and have a family but with who,
And who, who teaches them to write and be free,
The same person that says there is pain and suffering,
There is no hoping and cursing, no eating or sleeping,
We have those people in the world, our great Canadian soldiers,
And when do we hear about it,
When the media wants to hear about it,
They can make a difference they have made a difference alone with all the other soldiers,
Now we need someone to do the same for the bloodied and broken,
Physically and emotionally helpfully and open heartedly,
Like a soldier on the battlefield of broken hearts and homeless people,
Fighting the starvation and deprivation,
With a genuine means of killing our own 3rd world country,
The one in our own backyard in our own great nation,
Because I believe we can have love with no hate,
Because it will come eventually no matter how late,
Because I believe we will have light with no dark,
This is the time, it's the part in that movie this is an art,
To start and to play that harp that will end this war fully,
And it takes skill and the undying will of all that is good and holy,
For us to all be equal so we can have a sequel,

To live, in life, for the god of the blade and the knife,
To burn in hell with Hades and to pay thee,
For all the killing and murder, do you understand your evil orders,
Now we sacrifice soldiers, to your evil orders,
Sending them out to die, but what if they come back alive,
Trying to save you, me, and everyone else,
Not just in our good nation but in all the world's nations,
Good and bad because that's who we are, we are human
DO SOMETHING TO BETTER THE WORLD, YOURSELF.

Aprés Dedication

Life is full of light, but sometimes we can't see it for the shadows. Walk between the shadows, live in the light and love will find a way to make all things possible. Family is more important than you realize when you are young. Sometimes it is not always the family you are born with, but the one you adopt on your trip through life.

Thank you to Fred and Jill for being my "mom and dad" when I needed you most. You are the other part of family that has helped keep me sane when darkness threatened.

I love you both.

Hugs and prayers to all
Your cowboy.